HOTEL DESIGN

daab

Architects / Designers	Location	City	Page
Introduction			4
3meta.märklstetter + fischer	25 Hours Hotel	Hamburg	8
Arquitectonica	Le Meridien Cyberport	Hong Kong	16
Babylon Design	Chateau de Massillan	Uchaux	26
Gautam Bathia, Navin Gupta & Rajiv Saini	Devi Garh	Udaipur	32
BHPS Architekten	Radisson SAS	Berlin	42
Bilkey Llinas Design & Skidmore Owens & Merrill of London	Grand Hyatt Mumbai	Mumbai	46
Michele Bonan	Continentale	Florence	54
Ana Borallo, Aparicio Associates, Alexander Hutchison, In Sintu Designs & LeMoyne Lapointe Magne Architects	Hotel St. Paul	Montreal	60
Adalberto Campos	Hotel Cipriani	Punta del Este	66
Lesley Carstens & Silvio Rech, Architecture	North Island	North Island	72
Manuel Cervantes, Central de Arquitectura, Moisés Ison & José Sánchez	Deseo	Playa del Carmen	80
Chada Siembieda & Remedios Inc., Three Architecture	Raffles L'Ermitage	Los Angeles	90
Guido Ciompi	The Gray	Milan	96
Antonio Citterio & Partners	Bulgari Hotel	Milan	104
Conran Design	The Park Bangalore	Bangalore	112
Denton Corker, Marshall Group	Alila Jakarta	Jakarta	118
Matali Crasset	Hi Hotel	Nice	126
Cristina Gabas	Neri	Barcelona	132
Graft Architekten, Lars Krückeberg & Thomas Willemeit	Q!	Berlin	140
Nicole Grandsire & Patrick Le Villair	Ksar Char Bagh	Marrakech	148
Groupe H, Arch. Hervé Dessimoz	Crowne Plaza	Geneva	156
Kerry Hill Architects & Laurent Mondet	Amansara	Siem Reap	162
Kerrz Hill	The Sentosa Resort & Spa	Singapore	168
Hirsh, Bedner & Associates	The Park Hotel Chennai	Chennai	174
Kurt Hoffman Architects	Palafitte	Neuchatel	180
Kanko Kikaku Seddeisha	M Hotel	Singapore	188
Kaplan McLaughlin Diaz & Studio GAIA	W Hotel Mexico City	Mexico City	204
Dale Keller	Gran Hotel La Florida	Barcelona	212

Architects / Designers	Location	City	Page
Franziska & Daniel Kessler, Lemongrass Design Studio, Vogt & Weizenegger	Ku'damm 101 Hotel	Berlin	218
King Roselli Architetti	Es Hotel	Rome	224
Klein Heller, Vasilis Rodatos, Kathryn KNG	Life Gallery	Athens	230
	Metropolitan	Bangkok	240
Koning-Eizenberg	The Standard Downtown	Los Angeles	248
Heinz Legler & Veronique Lièvre	Verana	Puerto Vallarta	258
Meryanne Loum-Martin	Jnane Tamsna	Marrakech	264
Richard Martinet	Hotel de la Trémoille	Paris	270
Ingibjörg S. Pálmadóttir	101 Hotel	Reykjavik	276
Jean Pfaff, Romero & Schaefle, & Günther Vogt Eric Raffy	Greulich	Zurich	282
	Clinton South Beach	Miami	288
Karim Rashid	Semiramis	Athens	296
Pedro Rosario & Design Works, Annie Salgas	Water Club	San Juan	300
RTKL Associates of Dallas	Mandarin Oriental Miami	Miami	306
Lu Shien-Chieh	United Hotel	Taipei	314
Tei Shuwa Intentionallities & Tomato Design	Claska	Tokyo	322
Eren Talu	Hillside Su Hotel	Antalya	330
Fredrich Thomas	Park Hotel Tokyo	Tokyo	340
Matteo Thun	Vigilius Mountain Resort	Lana	346
Adam D. Tihany	The Aleph	Rome	352
Edward Tuttle	Park Hyatt Paris	Paris	360
	Amanjena	Marrakech	366
T.Y Wu, Wu's Deco	Les Suites Taipei	Taipei	372
Yabu Pushelberg	W Los Angeles Westwood	Los Angeles	378
	W Hotel Times Square	New York	384
Peter Zumthor	Therme Vals	Vals	390

Index 398
Imprint 400

Les mentalités changent depuis dix ans dans l'architecture et la décoration des hôtels, et cette tendance s'est amplifiée dans un passé tout récent. Ce ne sont plus maintenant quelques hôteliers aussi créatifs qu'isolés, mais des chaînes hôtelières entières et leurs investisseurs qui découvrent que l'architecture et le design sont un élément essentiel de leur acceptation par la clientèle, donc de la réussite des projets hôteliers. Leur design contemporain s'oriente à nouveau plus fortement sur le classicisme moderne et instaure un équilibre entre la construction, la fonction et l'esthétique. L'art en tant qu'expression individuelle poétisée et les structures high tech sous forme de matériaux nouveaux ou de configurations internes en réseaux intelligents coexistent désormais de plus en plus étroitement. Des exemples vecteurs de sens et en définitive porteurs de réussite s'orientent ce faisant sur les besoins d'un public d'hôtes rajeuni. L'enveloppe que représente un hôtel doit non seulement admettre les univers émotionnels propres au style de vie moderne, mais encore en capter tous les détails et les affiner. Cette affirmation se vérifie uniquement si l'on adopte une démarche intégrale qui inclut aussi bien les mises en scènes lumineuses, les techniques domotiques, le choix des matériaux, la définition des formes et des teintes, que l'ameublement assorti, spécialement dessiné dans ce but par les concepteurs comme le montrent de nombreux exemples. Bravant la mondialisation et son uniformisation stylistique, les démarches de décoration différentes, illustrées par plus de 50 exemples, attirent l'attention et répondent souvent à des motifs très personnels. Ces exemples livrent un aperçu complet de l'évolution internationale vécue par le design hôtelier au cours de ces 4 à 5 dernières années et mettent aussi en évidence, à travers toute la richesse d'inspiration de ces études, le point de départ commun à toutes ces activités architecturales et décoratives : créer un espace d'habitation, pour un temps.

In den letzten 10 Jahren und verstärkt in allerjüngster Zeit vollzieht sich bei der Gestaltung von Hotels ein Bewusstseinswandel. Nicht nur mehr vereinzelte, innovative Hoteliers, sondern inzwischen auch große Ketten und deren Investoren entdecken Architektur und Design als zentralen Bestandteil für die Akzeptanz und damit den Erfolg von Hotelprojekten. Zeitgenössisches Hoteldesign orientiert sich dabei wieder stark an der modernen Klassik und setzt auf die Balance aus Konstruktion, Funktion und Ästhetik. Kunst in Form einer individuellen, poetischen Ausdrucksweise und High Tech in Form neuartiger Werkstoffe oder intelligenter Inhouse-Vernetzungen finden dabei zu einer immer engeren Koexistenz. Sinnbringende und letztlich erfolgreiche Beispiele orientieren sich dabei an den Bedürfnissen der verjüngten Gästeschar. Die Hülle Hotel muss die emotionalen Welten des modernen Lebensstils nicht nur zulassen können, sondern mit all ihren Details aufnehmen und verfeinern. Dies funktioniert nur mit einem ganzheitlichen Ansatz, der Lichtinszenierungen, Haustechnik, Materialauswahl bzw. Form- und Farbgebung genauso einschließt, wie die passende Möblierung – in vielen Beispielen von den Designern eigens entworfen. Trotz Globalisierung und einer stilistischen Vereinheitlichung auffallend sind die unterschiedlichen, oftmals sehr persönlich motivierten Gestaltungsansätze in den hier präsentierten, über 50 Beispielen. Sie geben einen umfassenden Einblick in die internationale Entwicklung von Hoteldesign in den letzten 4-5 Jahren und zeigen bei der ganzen Vielfalt der Entwürfe immer auch den gemeinsamen Ausgangspunkt der Gestaltungsaufgabe: Die Schaffung von Wohnraum auf Zeit.

Combining the echoes of a minimalistic expression, the language of design hotel's composition appears to be deliberately simplified to offer the possibility of communication between the worlds of architectural design and industry. They are now moving closer together to enable the exchange of roles and defining the most sophisticated attainable qualities for a space and its users. Design concepts grew out of the 'art and tech' design; designing the connection of both necessities of being connected to the world physically and cybernetically, in most cases; moreover, integrating individuals from a conventional perceptual experience into a contemporary mood. This contemporary language is also reflected on the distinctive lightning, purpose designer furniture and in the use of different materials; discovered within the same context and the innovative ones that adapt themselves to the global corporate culture. The combination of ethnic and traditional design in the same way transports itself into this new wave of modern and timeless expression; in order, to persist through time and space. The harmonious existence of this type of hotels emerged world wide five years ago, allowing inhabitants to adapt a new identity through the experiences of architectonic spaces and cosmopolitan hubs. The volume at hand illustrates over 50 contemporary international design examples that naturally fuse through the balance of comfort, function and style, making hotels a "home in time".

Combinando los ecos de una expresión minimalista, el lenguaje de la composición de los hoteles de diseño aparenta estar deliberadamente simplificado para ofrecer la posibilidad de comunicación entre los mundos de diseño arquitectural e industrial. Ahora en día acercándose más para permitir el intercambio y desempeño de papeles y así poder definir las cualidades mas sofisticadas de un espacio y de sus respectivos usuarios. Los conceptos de diseño nacieron del diseño del 'arte y la tecnología'; diseñando la conexión de ambas necesidades de estar conectados al mundo físicamente y cibernéticamente, en la mayoría de los casos; además, integrando a los individuos de una experiencia convencional y perspicaz a una disposición con temporal. Este lenguaje con temporal también es reflejado en las distintas formas de iluminación, los determinados muebles de diseño y en el uso de diferentes materiales; descubiertos en el mismo contexto y los innovadores que se adaptan a la cultura de corporación global. La combinación de diseño ético y tradicional de igual forma se transporta por si mismo hacia este nuevo movimiento de expresión moderna e indefinido tiempo; para así poder persistir a través del tiempo y espacio. La existencia armoniosa de este tipo de hoteles se introdujo en la ultimos cinco años alrededor del mundo, permitiendo a los habitantes la opción de adaptar una nueva identidad a través de las experiencias de espacios arquitectónicos y centros cosmopolita nos. El volumen en mano, ilustra más de 50 ejemplos de diseño internacional con temporal que naturalmente fusionan a través del balance de comodidad, función y estilo, convirtiendo a los hoteles en una "casa en un determinado tiempo".

Durante gli ultimi 10 anni e maggiormente in tempi recentissimi si sta verificando un cambiamento nel modo di percepire la creazione di alberghi. Non soltanto singoli albergatori innovativi, ma nel frattempo anche grandi catene ed i loro investori scoprono l'architettura ed il design quali componenti essenziali per essere accettati e quindi per garantire il successo degli hotel progettati. Il design contemporaneo degli hotel ritorna ad orientarsi fortemente sul classico moderno e punta sull'equilibrio tra costruzione, funzionalità ed estetica. L'arte sotto forma di un modo d'espressione individuale e poetico ed il high tech sotto forma di materiali costruttivi innovativi o un'interoperatività interna intelligente si ritrovano a coesistere in modo sempre più stretto. Esempi significativi ed infine di successo si orientano sui fabbisogni di una clientela più giovane. L'hotel come involucro non deve soltanto far entrare i mondi emozionali dello stile moderno di vita, ma anche includere e raffinare tutti i suoi dettagli. Ciò funziona soltanto con un approccio integrato che comprende la messa in scena dell'illuminazione, gli impianti dell'edificio, la scelta dei materiali, delle forme e dei colori così come l'arredamento adatto – in molti casi creato appositamente dallo stilista. Si mettono in evidenza - nonostante la globalizzazione e l'uniformazione stilistica - i diversi e spesso personalissimi approcci al modo di creare, presentati qui con oltre 50 esempi. Permettono di prendere in esame lo sviluppo internazionale al livello del design di hotel durante gli ultimi 4 a 5 anni e con tutta la varietà delle creazioni dimostrano sempre il punto di partenza in comune del processo creativo: la creazione di uno spazio abitativo temporaneo.

3META, EVI MÄERKLSTETTER + FISCHER | MUNICH
FREIRAUM & LEBENSART AG | AUGSBURG
25 hours hotel
Hamburg, Germany | 2003

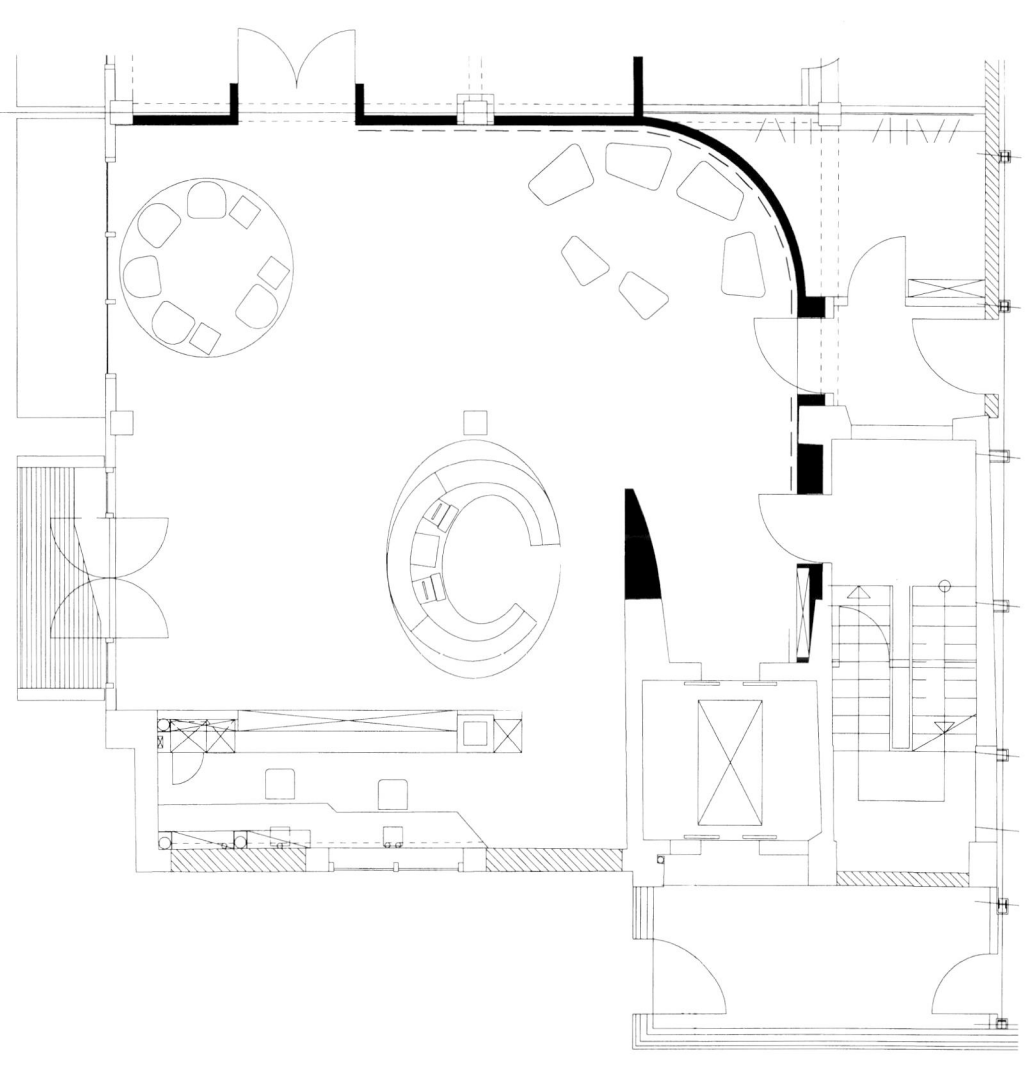

ARQUITECTONICA | MIAMI
Le Meridien Cyberport
Hong Kong | 2004

BABYLON DESIGN | LONDON
Chateau de Massillan
Uchaux, France | 2002

GAUTAM BATHIA | UDAIPUR
NAVIN GUPTA | NEW DELHI
RAJIV SAINI | MUMBAI
Devi Garh
Udaipur, India | 2000

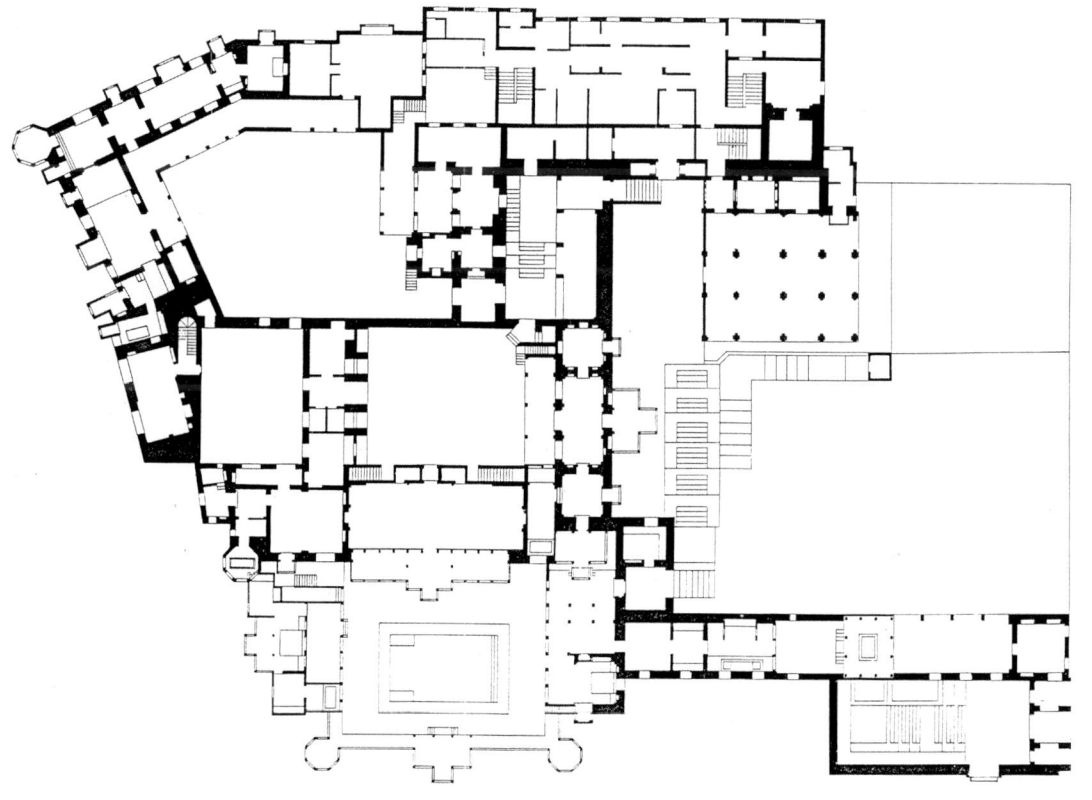

BHPS ARCHITEKTEN | BERLIN
Radisson SAS
Berlin, Germany | 2004

BILKEY LINAS DESIGN | CHICAGO
SKIDMORE OWENS & MERRILL | LONDON
Grand Hyatt Mumbai
Mumbai, India | 2004

MICHELE BONAN | FLORENCE
Continentale
Florence, Italy | 2003

ANA BORALLO | MONTREAL
CARLOS APARICIO ASSOCIATES | NEW YORK
IN SITU DESIGN | NEW YORK
LEMOYNE LAPOINTE MAGNE ARCHITECTS | CHICAGO
Hotel St. Paul
Montreal, Canada | 2001

ADALBERTO CAMPOS | PUNTA DEL ESTE
Hotel Cipriani
Punta del Este, Uruguay | 2004

LESLEY CARSTENS & SILVIO RECH ARCHITECTURE | JOHANNESBURG
North Island
North Island, Seychelles | 2003

CENTRAL DE ARQUITECTURA | MEXICO CITY
MANUEL CERVANTES, MOISÉS ISON, JOSÉ SÁNCHEZ
Deseo
Playa del Carmen, Mexico | 2002

CHHADA SIEMBIEDA & REMEDIOS INC. | LOS ANGELES
THREE ARCHITECTURE | DALLAS
Raffles L'Ermitage
Beverly Hills, USA | 2000

GUIDO CIOMPI | FLORENCE
The Gray
Milan, Italy | 2003

ANTONIO CITTERIO | MILAN
Bulgari Hotel
Milan, Italy | 2004

CONRAN DESIGN GROUP | LONDON
The Park Bangalore
Bangalore, India | 2000

DENTON CORKER MARSHALL GROUP | MELBOURNE
Alila Jakarta
Jakarta, Indonesia | 2000

MATALI CRASSET | PARIS
Hi Hotel
Nice, France | 2003

CRISTINA GABÁS | BARCELONA
Hotel Neri
Barcelona, Spain | 2003

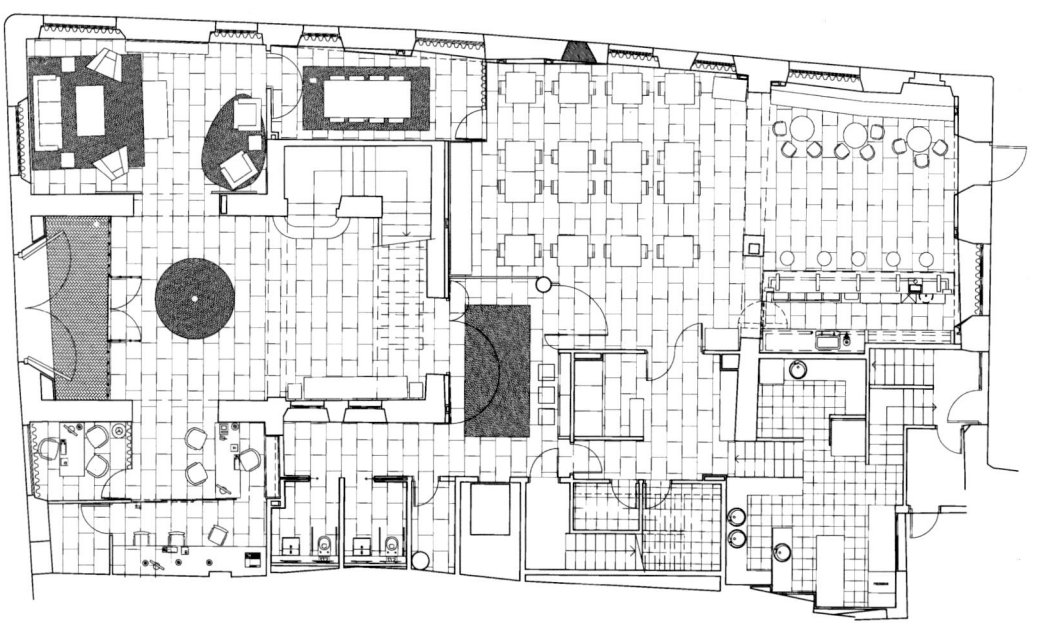

GRAFT ARCHITEKTEN | BERLIN LOS ANGELES
LARS KRÜCKEBERG, WOLFRAM PÜTZ,
THOMAS WILLEMEIT
Q!
Berlin, Germany | 2004

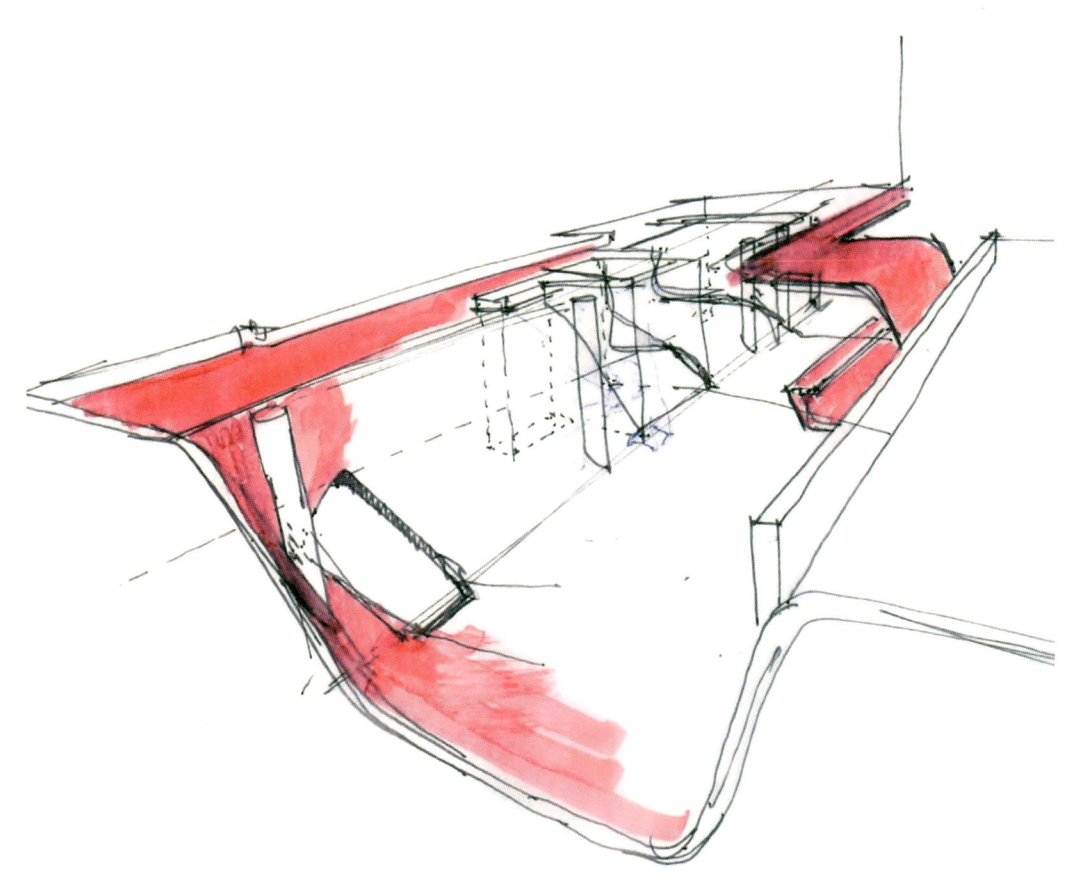

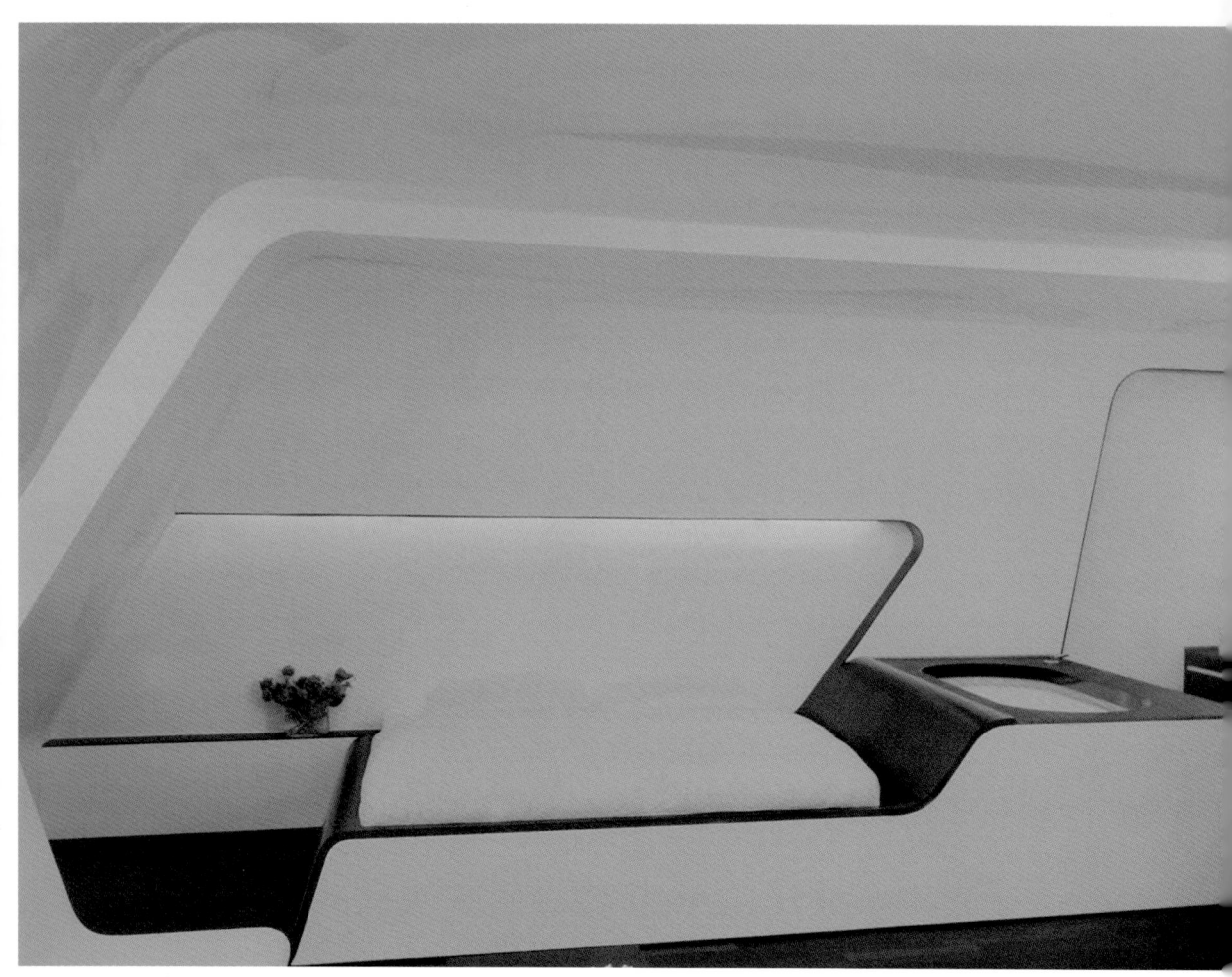

NICOLE GRANDSIRE & PATRICK LE VILLAIR | MARRAKECH
Ksar Char Bagh
Marrakech, Marocco | 2003

GROUPE H, ARCH. HERVÈ DESSIMOZ | GENEVA
Crowne Plaza
Geneva, Switzerland | 2003

KERRY HILL ARCHITECTS | SINGAPORE
LAURENT MONDET | PARIS
Amansara
Siem Reap, Cambodia | 2003

KERRY HILL ARCHITECTS | SINGAPORE
The Sentosa Resort & Spa
Singapore | 2003

HIRSH, BEDNER & ASSOCIATES | LOS ANGELES
The Park Hotel Chennai
Chennai, India | 2002

KURT HOFFMAN ARCHITECTS | LAUSANNE
Palafitte
Neuchatel, Switzerland | 2002

KANKO KIKAKU SEKKEISHA | SINGAPORE
M Hotel
Singapore | 2002

KAPLAN MCLAUGHLIN DIAZ | MEXICO CITY
STUDIO GAIA | NEW YORK
W Hotel Mexico City
Mexico City, Mexico | 2004

DALE KELLER | BARCELONA
Gran Hotel La Florida
Barcelona, Spain | 2003

FRANZISKA & DANIEL KESSLER | ZURICH
LEMONGRASS DESIGN STUDIO | BERLIN
VOGT & WEIZENEGGER | BERLIN
Ku'damm 101
Berlin, Germany | 2003

KING ROSELLI ARCHITETTI | ROME
Es Hotel
Rome, Italy | 2000

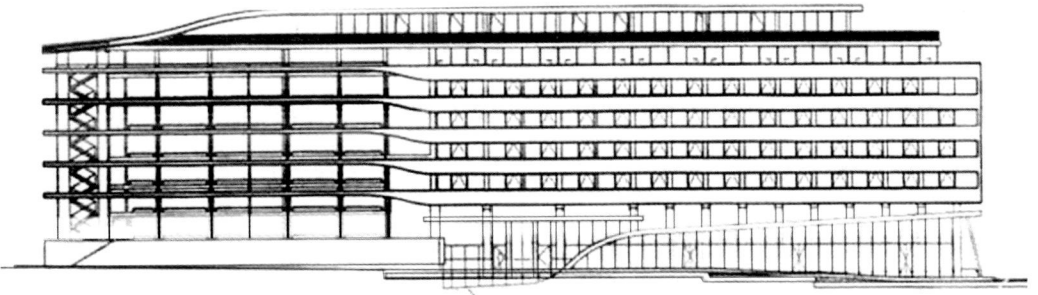

KLEIN & HALLER | DUSSELDORF
VASILIS RODATOS | ATHENS
Life Gallery
Athens, Greece | 2004

KATHRYN KNG | SINGAPORE
The Metropolitan
Bangkok, Thailand | 2004

KONING-EIZENBERG ARCHITECTURE | LOS ANGELES
The Standard Downtown
Los Angeles, USA | 2002

HEINZ LEGLER & VERONIQUE LIÈVRE | LOS ANGELES
Verana
Puerto Vallarta, Mexico | 2000

MERYANNE LOUM-MARTIN | MARRAKECH
Jnane Tamsna
Marrakech, Marocco | 2001

RICHARD MARTINET | PARIS
Hotel de la Trémoille
Paris, France | 2002

INGIBJÖRG PÁLMADÓTTIR | REYKJAVIK
101 Hotel
Reykjavik, Iceland | 2002

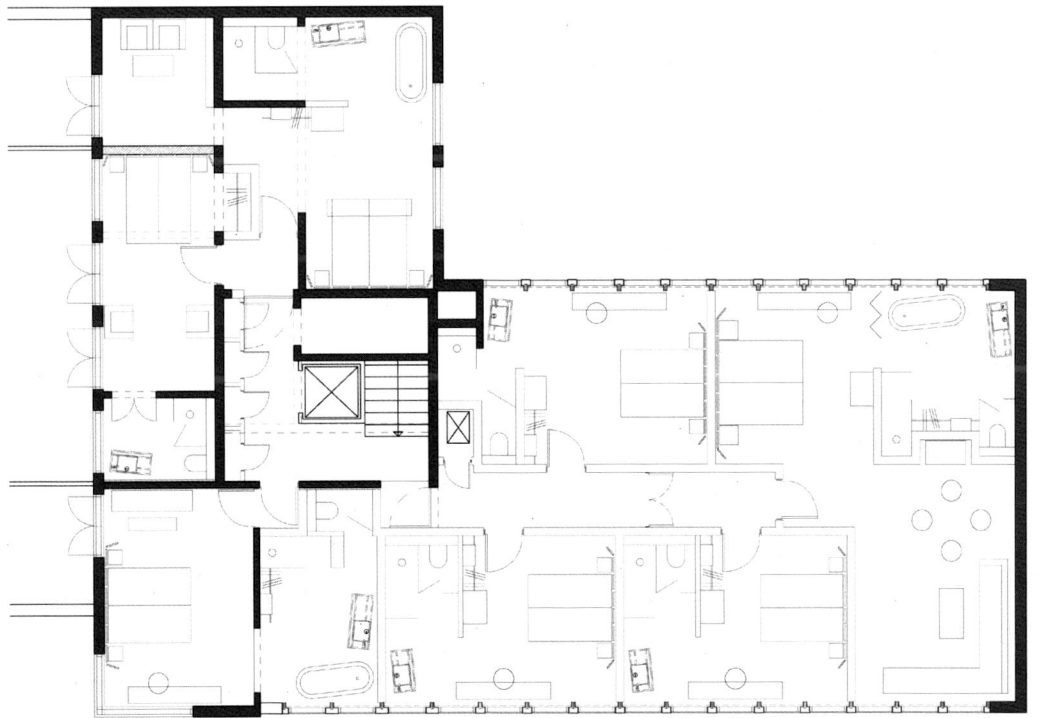

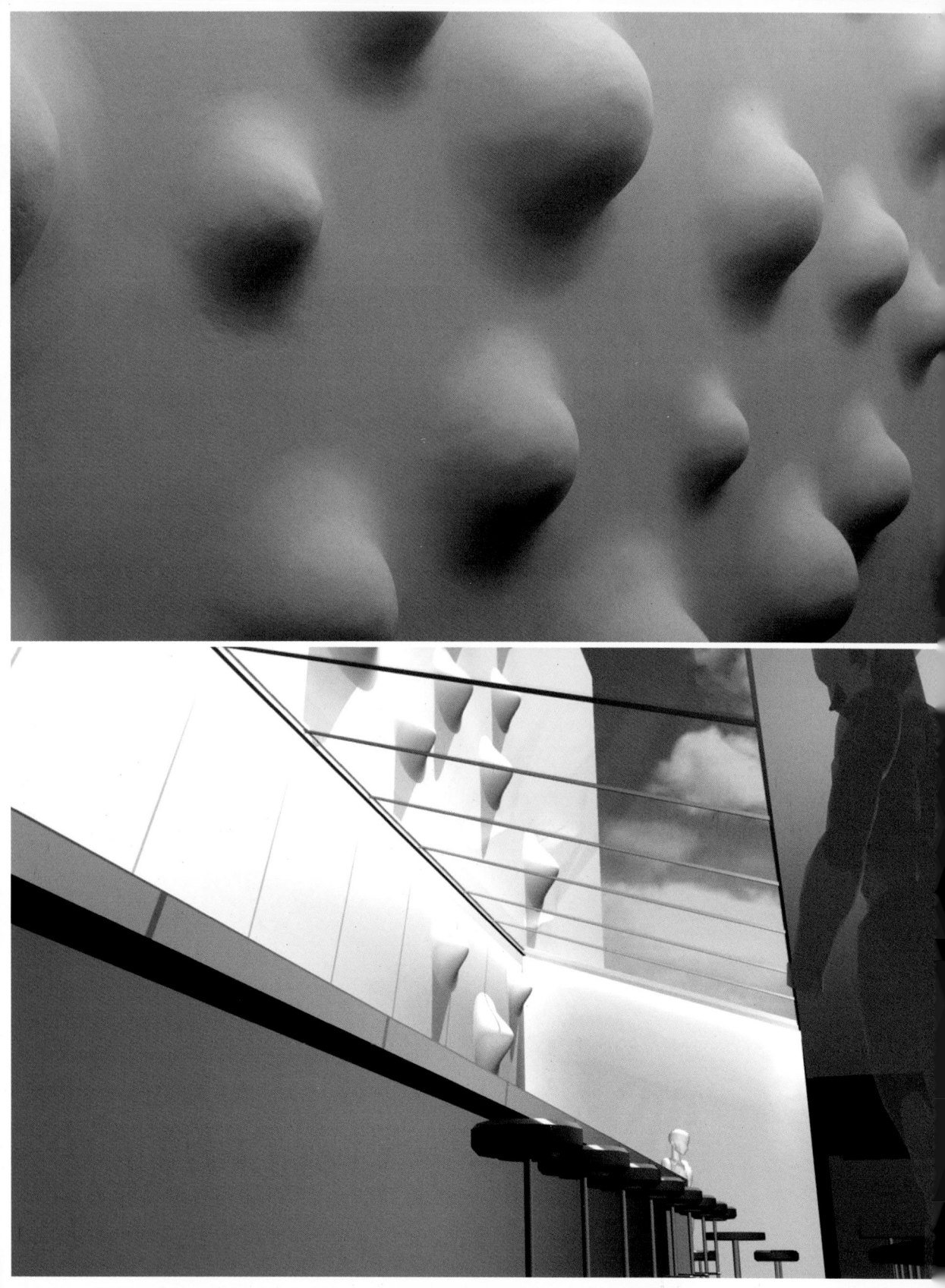

JEAN PFAFF, ROMERO & SCHAEFLE, GÜNTHER VOGT | ZURICH
Greulich
Zurich, Switzerland | 2003

ERIC RAFFY | PARIS
Clinton South Beach
Miami, USA | 2003

KARIM RASHID | NEW YORK
Semiramis
Athens, Greece | 2004

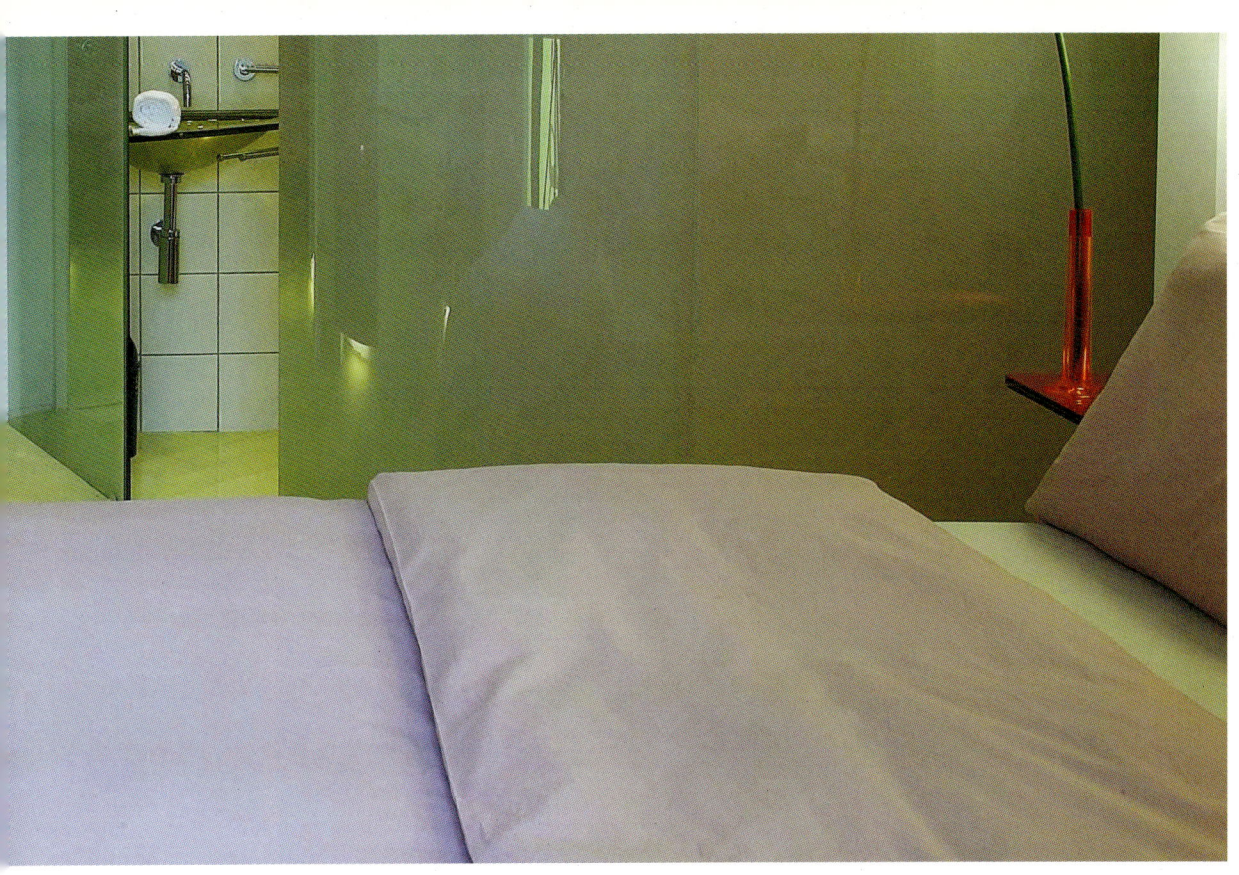

PEDRO ROSARIO & DESIGN WORKS | SAN JUAN
ANNIE SALGAS | SAN JUAN
Water Club
San Juan, Puerto Rico | 2001

RTKL ASSOCIATES | DALLAS
Mandarin Oriental
Miami, USA | 2000

LU SHIEN-CHIEH | TAIPEI
United Hotel
Taipei, Taiwan | 2000

TEI SHUWA INTENTIONALLITIES | TOKYO
TOMATO DESIGN | LONDON
Claska
Tokyo, Japan | 2002

EREN TALU | ANTALYA
Hillside Su Hotel
Antalya, Turkey | 2003

FREDRIC THOMAS | PARIS
Park Hotel Tokyo
Tokyo, Japan | 2003

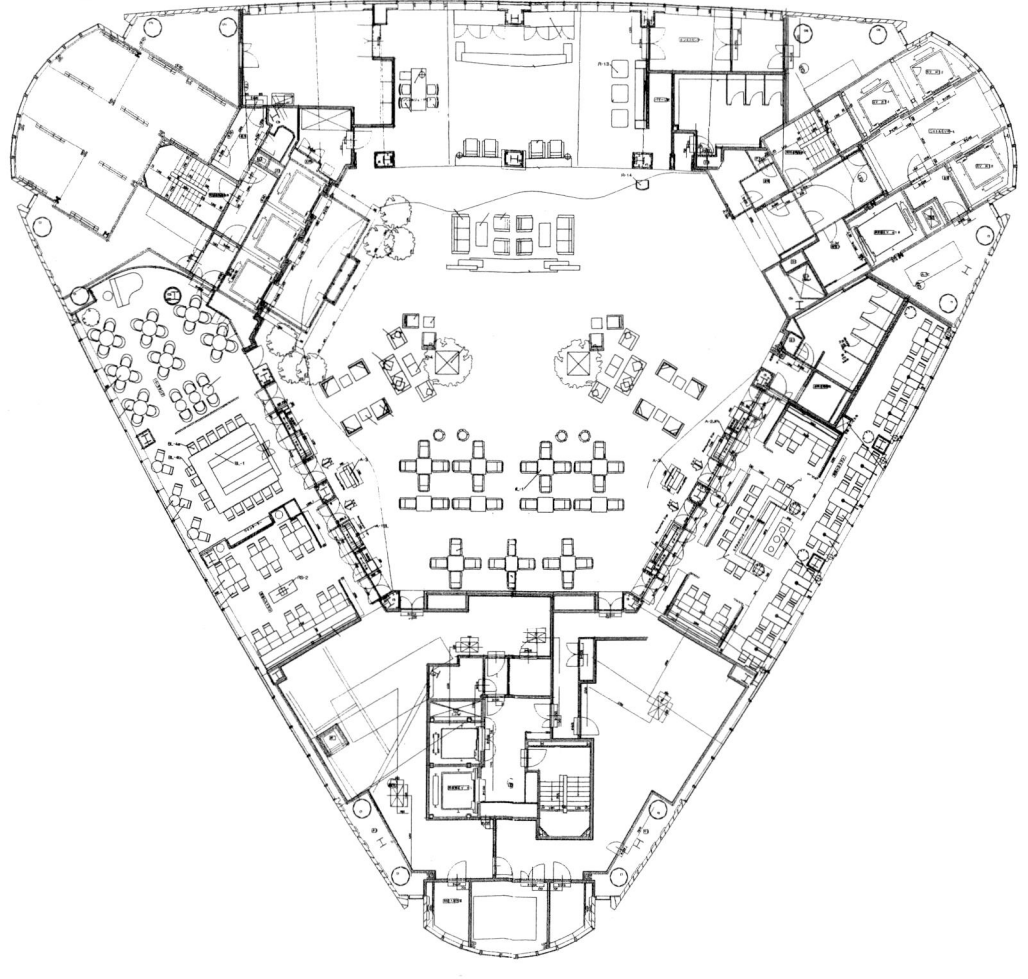

MATTEO THUN | MILAN
Vigilius Mountain Resort
Lana, Italy | 2003

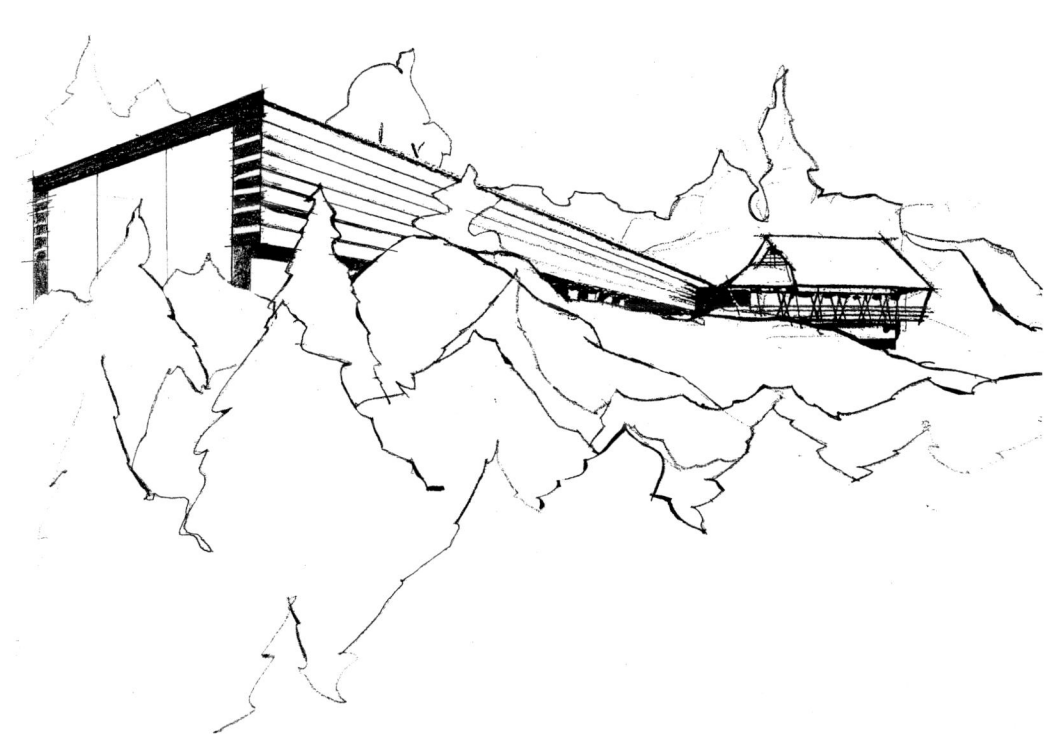

ADAM D. TIHANY | NEW YORK
The Aleph
Rome, Italy | 2003

EDWARD TUTTLE | PARIS
Park Hyatt Paris
Paris , France | 2002

EDWARD TUTTLE | PARIS
Amanjena
Marrakech, Marocco | 2000

T. Y WU. WU'S DECO | TAIPEI
Les Suites Taipei
Taipei, Taiwan | 2003

YABU PUSHELBERG | NEW YORK
W Los Angeles Westwood
Los Angeles, USA | 2002

YABU PUSHELBERG | NEW YORK
W Hotel Times Square
New York, USA | 2002

PETER ZUMTHOR | HALDENSTEIN
Therme Vals
Vals, Switzerland | 1998

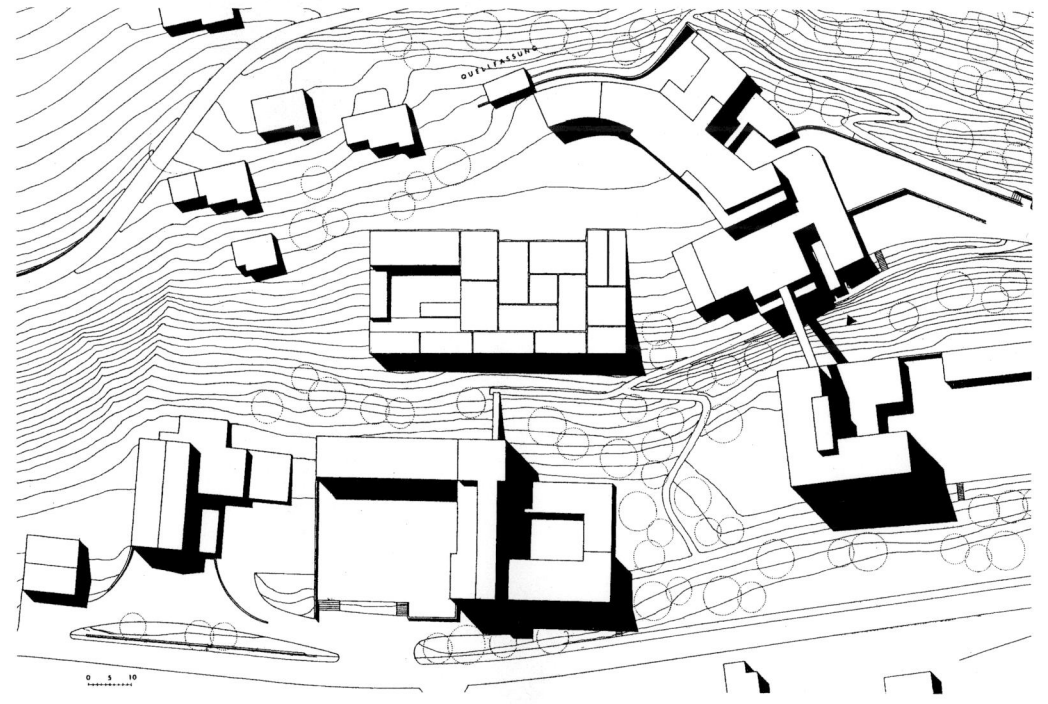

Index

3meta.evi mäerklstetter + fischer, Munich
25 Hours Hotel, Hamburg — 8

Carlos Aparicio Associates, New York
Hotel St. Paul, Montreal — 60

Arquitectonica, Miami
www.arquitectonica.com
Le Meridien Cyberport, Hong Kong — 16

Babylon Design, London
www.babylonlondon.com
Chateau de Massillan, Uchaux — 26

Gautam Bathia, Udaipur
Devi Garh, Udaipur — 32

BHPS Architekten, Berlin
www.bhps-architekten.de
Radisson SAS, Berlin — 42

Bilkey Linas Design, Chicago
Grand Hyatt Mumbai — 46

Michele Bonan, Florence
Continentale, Florence — 54

Ana Borallo, Montreal
Hotel St. Paul, Montreal — 60

Adalberto Campos, Punta del Este
Hotel Cipriani, Punta del Este — 66

Lesley Carstens & Silvio Rech Architecture, Johannesburg
North Island, Seychelles — 72

Central de Arquitectura, Mexico City
Manuel Cervantes, Moisés Ison & José Sánchez
Deseo, Playa del Carmen — 80

Chhada Siembieda & Remedios Inc., Los Angeles
Raffles L'Ermitage, Los Angeles — 90

Guido Ciompi, Florence
The Gray, Milan — 96

Antonio Citterio & Partners, Milan
www.antonio-citterio.it
Bulgari, Milan — 104

Conran Design Group, London
www.conrandesigngroup.com
The Park Bangalore — 112

Denton Corker Marshall Group, Melbourne
Alila Jakarta — 118

Matali Crasset, Paris
www.matalicrasset.com
Hi Hotel, Nice — 126

Cristina Gabás, Barcelona
Hotel Neri, Barcelona — 132

Studio GAIA, New York
W Hotel Mexico City — 204

Navin Gupta, New Delhi
Devi Garh, Udaipur — 32

Graft Architekten, Berlin Los Angeles
Lars Krückeberg, Wolfram Pütz, Thomas Willemeit
www.graftlab.com
Q!, Berlin — 140

Nicole Grandsire & Patrick Le Villair, Marrakech
Ksar Char Bagh, Marrekech — 148

Groupe H, Arch. Hervé Dessimoz, Geneva
Crowne Plaza, Geneva — 156

Kerry Hill Architects, Singapore
Amansara, Siem Reap — 162
The Sentosa Resort & Spa, Singapore — 168

Hirsh, Bedner & Associates, Los Angeles
The Park Hotel Chennai — 174
www.hbadesign.com

Kurt Hoffman Architects, Lausanne
Palafitte, Neuchatel — 180

Kanko Kikaku Sekkeisha, Singapore
M Hotel, Singapore — 188

In Situ Design, New York
LeMoyne Lapointe Magne Architects, Chicago
Hotel St. Paul, Montreal — 60

Kaplan McLaughlin Diaz, Mexico City
www.kmd-arch.com
W Hotel Mexico City — 204

Dale Keller, Barcelona
Gran Hotel La Florida, Barcelona — 212

Franziska & Daniel Kessler, Zurich
Ku'damm 101 Hotel, Berlin — 218

King Roselli Architettl, Rome
www.kingroselli.com
Es Hotel, Rome — 224

Klein & Haller, Dusseldorf
Life Gallery, Athens — 230

Kathryn KNG, Singapore
Metropolitan, Bangkok — 240

Koning-Eizenberg Architecture, Los Angeles
www.kearch.com
The Standard Downtown, Los Angeles — 248

Heinz Legler & Veronique Lièvre, Los Angeles
Verana, Puerto Vallarta — 258

Lemongrass Design Studio, Berlin
Ku'damm 101 Hotel, Berlin — 218

Meryanne Loum-Martin, Marrakech
Jnane Tamsna, Marrakech — 264

Richard Martinet, Paris
Hotel de la Trémoille, Paris — 270

Laurent Mondet, Paris
Amansara, Siem Reap — 162

Ingibjörg S. Pálmadóttir, Reykjavik
101 Hotel, Reykjavik — 276

Jean Pfaff, Zurich
Greulich, Zurich — 282

Eric Raffy, Paris
Clinton South Beach, Miami — 288

Karim Rashid, New York
www.karimrashid.com
Semiramis, Athens — 296

Vasilis Rodatos, Athens
Life Gallery, Athens — 230

Romero & Schaefle
Greulich, Zurich — 282

Pedro Rosario & Design Works, San Juan
Water Club, San Juan, Puerto Rico — 300

RTKL Associates, Dallas
www.rtkl.com
Mandarin Oriental Miami — 306

Rajiv Saini, Mumbai
Devi Garh, Udaipur — 32

Annie Salgas
Water Club, San Juan, Puerto Rico — 300

Lu Shien-Chieh, Taipei
United Hotel, Taipei — 314

Tei Shuwa Intentionallities, Tokyo
Claska, Tokyo — 322

Skidmore Owens & Merrill, London
Grand Hyatt Mumbai — 46

Eren Talu, Antalya
Hillside Su Hotel, Antalya — 330

Fredric Thomas, Paris
Park Hotel Tokyo — 340

Three Architecture, Dallas
Raffles L'Ermitage, Los Angeles — 90

Matteo Thun, Milan
www.matteothun.com
Vigilius Mountain Resort, Lana — 346

Adam D. Tihany, New York
www.tihanydesign.com
The Aleph, Rome — 352

Tomato Design, London
www.tomato.co.uk
Claska, Tokyo — 322

Edward Tuttle, Paris
Park Hyatt Paris — 360
Amanjena, Marrakech — 366

T.Y Wu, Wu's Deco, Taipei
Les Suites Taipei — 372

Günther Vogt, Zurich
Greulich, Zurich — 282

Vogt & Weizenegger, Berlin
Ku'damm 101 Hotel, Berlin — 218

Yabu Pushelberg, New York
www.yabupushelberg.com
W Los Angeles Westwood — 378
W Hotel Time Square, New York — 384

Peter Zumthor, Haldenstein
www.zumthor.ch
Therme Vals — 390

copyright © 2004 daab
cologne   london   new york

published and distributed worldwide by
daab gmbh
stadtwaldgürtel 57
d - 50935 köln

t +49-221-94 10 740
f +49-221-94 10 741

mail@daab-online.de
www.daab-online.de

publisher ralf daab
rdaab@daab-online.de

art director feyyaz
mail@feyyaz.com

editorial coordination patricia massó, ursula dietmair & joachmin fischer
introduction in english and spanish michelle galindo
german translation martin nicholas kunz
french translation dominique santoro, ade team
italian translation jacqueline rizzo, ade team
layout michelle galindo
prepress and imaging jan hausberg, susanne olbrich

photo credits (name page)
Courtesy 101 Hotel 276, Courtesy Amanresorts 162, Courtesy Babylon Design 26, Roland Bauer 32, 96, 148, 264, 270, 282, 288, 318, 334, 372, 378, 306, 322, 360, 366, 390, Courtesy Boscolo Hotels 352, Courtesy Bulgari 104, Santi Calca 224, Hotel Cipriani 66, Courtesy Como Hotels & Resorts 240, Evan Dion 384, Courtesy Ferragamo Hotels 54, Luigi Filatici 224, Groupe H 156, Courtesy Hillside Su 330, Kessler + Kessler 218, Jose King 224, Karin Kohlberg 60, Martin Nicholas Kunz 8, 16, 46, 72, 80, 90, 96, 118, 132, 168, 174, 180, 188, 212, 248, 300, 314, 340, 352, 372, 378, Heinz Legler 258, Courtesy Life Gallery 230, Philip Menser 42, Undine Prohl 80, Bharath Ramamrutham 112, 174, Fotostudio Dirk Schaper 140, Courtesy Semiramis 296, Uwe Spoering 126, Matteo Thun Studio 346, Lian Waisbrod 204

copyright © 2004 fusion publishing, www.fusion-publishing.com

printed in spain
Anman Gràfiques del Vallès, Spain
www.anman.com

isbn 3-937718-05-2
d.l.: B-41.024.04

all rights reserved.
no part of this publication may be reproduced in any manner.